Baby Blocks

A Baby Shower Game

by

Dorinda C. McCombs

DORRANCE PUBLISHING CO., INC.
PITTSBURGH, PENNSYLVANIA 15222

ISBN # 0-8059-4023-5
Printed in the United States of America

First Printing

For information or to order additional books, please write:
Dorrance Publishing Co., Inc.
643 Smithfield Street
Pittsburgh, Pennsylvania 15222
U.S.A.

DEDICATED TO ALL OF MY SISTER-FRIENDS AND ESPECIALLY DILCIE'S BABY

BABY BLOCKS RULES: THERE ARE NO RULES!
HAVE LOTS OF FUN WITH THIS GAME BOOK AND LAUGH A LOT!

NOTES TO HOSTESS:
IT IS SUGGESTED THAT THE HOSTESS READ THE GAME BOOK BEFORE THE ACTUAL PARTY TIME! THIS WILL LET YOU KNOW WHEN TO USE THE ITEMS NEEDED.

EACH PAGE IS ONE CATEGORY. THERE IS A CATEGORY CHART FOR EACH PLAYER AT THE BACK OF THE BOOK. YOU CAN HAVE ANY NUMBER OF GUESTS PLAY "BABY BLOCKS." IF YOU HAVE A SMALL NUMBER OF GUESTS, YOU MAY WISH TO PUT A TIME LIMIT ON THE GAME. IT COULD GO ON FOR HOURS! GIFTS ARE UP TO THE HOSTESS. YOU CAN GIVE ONE GIFT TO THE GUEST WITH THE MOST BABY DOLLARS OR THE TOP THREE. THERE IS ONE CATEGORY WHICH IS AN AUTOMATIC GIFT. YOU MAY CHOOSE TO ALLOW THE MOTHER-TO-BE TO OPEN ONE OF HER GIFTS OR GIVE AWAY A GIFT TO THE GUEST.

ITEMS NEEDED ARE TWO BABY ITEMS (LOTION, POWDER), THREE PLASTIC CUPS, COOKED OATMEAL, APPLESAUCE, FLOUR, PENCILS, A PICTURE OF A PIECE OF BABY FURNITURE, COTTON BALLS, A BOWL, A SCARF, YOU DO NOT NEED TO BUY ALL OF THESE ITEMS, SEVERAL OF THEM CAN BE SUBSTITUTED FOR WHAT YOU ALREADY HAVE IN YOUR CABINETS!!! READ THE BOOK AHEAD OF TIME!

TO BEGIN:
HAVE THE MOTHER-TO-BE CHOOSE A CATEGORY AT RANDOM... (YES SHE CAN PLAY TOO!) WHEN A GUEST CHOOSES A RANDOM CATEGORY, FLIP TO THE PAGE WITH THAT BLOCK ON IT. READ THE VALUE OF THE BLOCK "OUT LOUD" FOR THE GUESTS. IF A QUESTION IS FIRST, THE PERSON JUST ANSWERS THE QUESTION. IF AN ANSWER IS FIRST, THE PERSON MUST SAY THEIR RESPONSE IN QUESTION FORM!

WHEN THE GUEST ANSWERS CORRECTLY, THEY GET THE DOLLAR VALUE OF THE BABY BLOCK AND SHOULD WRITE IT ON THEIR TALLY SHEET. MOVE ON TO THE NEXT GUEST AND ALLOW THEM TO CHOOSE ANOTHER RANDOM CATEGORY. THERE IS NO ORDER TO THE CATEGORIES.   UPON COMPLETING ALL OF THE CATEGORIES OR RUNNING OUT OF YOUR CHOSEN TIME LIMIT, TOTAL ALL TALLY SHEETS AND CHOOSE YOUR WINNERS! TALLY SHEETS ARE PROVIDED AT THE BACK OF THE BOOK ALONG WITH THE CATEGORY SHEETS FOR EACH GUEST.

THANKS FOR PLAYING BABY BLOCKS!

TOYS	LOVE	RELIGIOUS	NURSERY	CHILDREN'S BOOKS	TEENAGER
2	MEDITA-TION	L	FRIENDS	BOTTLES	LAYETTE
FORMULA	GRANDMA	HOSPITAL	WILD	SHOTS	PEDIA-TRICIAN
ARTS	?	STRESS	SLEEP	CULTURE	S
P	FOOD	TODDLER	NAMES	HEIGHT AND WEIGHT	CAR SEATS
BABY-SITTER	DAY CARE	WILD	T	DAD	SEX
ALLERGIES	HELP!	LOANS	DAY OUTING	STROLLER	GIRL
OVERNIGHT	EQUIP-MENT	BOY	D	BILLS	CLOTHING

CATEGORY: TOYS FOR $100

ANSWER:
THE AGE THAT A CHILD CAN PLAY WITH
SOFT BLOCKS.

QUESTION:
WHAT IS 6 MONTHS?

CATEGORY: LOVE FOR $300

MAKE EVERYONE REPEAT AFTER YOU!
"POSITIVE REINFORCEMENT IS SOMETHING
WE ALL NEED. IT IS VITAL TO LET CHILDREN
KNOW HOW MUCH WE LOVE THEM. SO
TODAY, I WILL TAKE A MOMENT TO LET
SOMEONE YOUNG KNOW HOW I FEEL
ABOUT THEM!"

CATEGORY: RELIGIOUS FOR $100

ANSWER:
A RELIGIOUS CEREMONY FOR A BABY'S BIRTH.

QUESTION:
WHAT IS A CHRISTENING OR BRI?

CATEGORY: NURSERY FOR $100

QUESTION:
NAME THREE ITEMS FOUND IN A NURSERY.

ANSWER:
BASSINET/CRIB, BABY BATH, BABY SWING, DRESSER, CHANGING TABLE, DIAPER PAIL, DIAPER BAG, LAUNDRY HAMPER, PLAYPEN, ROCKING CHAIR, DIAPERS, CLOTHES.

CATEGORY: CHILDREN'S BOOKS FOR $100

QUESTION:
NAME A POPULAR CHILDREN'S BOOK.

EXAMPLES: 3 LITTLE PIGS, 3 BLIND MICE,
LITTLE RED RIDING HOOD, ADDY GOES TO
SCHOOL, ANANSI THE SPIDER, ETC.

CATEGORY: TEENAGER FOR $100

ANSWER:
CRITICAL QUESTIONS TO ASK A TEEN
BABYSITTER.

QUESTION:
HAVE YOU BABYSITTED BEFORE. DO YOU
HAVE ANY REFERENCES, HOW OLD WERE
THE CHILDREN YOU KEPT?

CATEGORY: 2 FOR $300

ANSWER:
THE MOST OFTEN USED WORD BY A TWO
YEAR OLD.

QUESTION:
WHAT IS " NO!" ?

CATEGORY: MEDITATIONS FOR $200

ANSWER:
TWO WAYS TO KEEP DAD AND MOM CALM
DURING CHILDBIRTH.

QUESTION:
WHAT ARE PREPARATION,
UNDERSTANDING, AND A POSITIVE
ATTITUDE?

CATEGORY: L FOR $500

"LEARN" HOW TO DRAW! HAVE THE LUCKY
PERSON SIT WITH THEIR BACK TO THE
MOTHER-TO-BE IN A CHAIR. GIVE THEM A
PIECE OF PAPER AND A CRAYON. THE
MOTHER TO BE HAS TO DESCRIBE PIECE
OF BABY FURNITURE. THE TRICK IS - THEY
CAN ONLY USE THESE WORDS:
 UP DOWN LEFT RIGHT TOP BOTTOM
CIRCLE SQUARE TRIANGLE RECTANGLE.

*NOTE TO HOSTESS: TIME LIMIT 3 MINUTES!

CATEGORY: FRIENDS FOR $200

QUESTION:
NAME TWO PEOPLE THE MOTHER-TO-BE
CAN CALL WHEN SHE IS READY TO
SCREAM!

ANSWER:
THERE SHOULD BE AT LEAST TWO IN THE
ROOM!

CATEGORY: BOTTLES FOR $100

ANSWER:
A TYPE OF BABY BOTTLE.

QUESTION:
WHAT IS GLASS, PLASTIC, OR
DISPOSABLE?

CATEGORY: LAYETTE FOR $100

QUESTION:
WHAT IS INCLUDED IN THE LAYETTE?

ANSWER:
DIAPERS, UNDERSHIRTS, GOWNS,
SWEATERS, BLANKETS,, BIBS, BOOTIES,
WASH CLOTHS, TOWELS, HOODED BATH
TOWEL, DIAPER BAG.

CATEGORY: FORMULA FOR $100

ANSWER:
ONE TYPE OF FORMULA.

QUESTION:
WHAT IS READY TO USE, CONCENTRATED, POWDER, OR SOY?

CATEGORY: GRANDMA FOR $500

FINISH SENTENCE. MOTHER KNOWS BEST
BUT GRANDMA...

ANSWER : KNOWS BETTER!

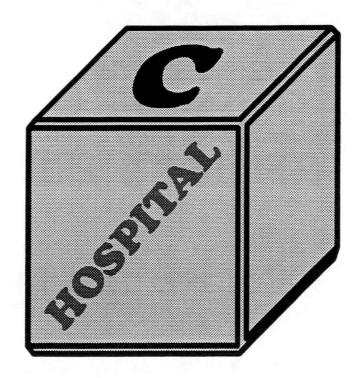

CATEGORY: HOSPITAL FOR $100

QUESTION:
NAME 3 THINGS TO TAKE TO THE
HOSPITAL.

ANSWER:
CAMERA, RECORDER, WASHCLOTH, LIP
BALM, SNACKS, MAGAZINE, PHONE
NUMBERS OF FAMILY AND FRIENDS, ROBE,
SLIPPERS, INSURANCE PAPERS, CAR SEAT.

CATEGORY: WILD
* PLACE A BET AND DOUBLE YOUR MONEY!
OR LOSE IT ALL ON THIS CATEGORY!

QUESTION:
LIST TEN WAYS IN WHICH WE CAN TEACH
LOVE, RESPECT, AND PRIDE
TO A CHILD WITHIN 60 SECONDS!

ANSWER: ANYTHING GOES!

CATEGORY: SHOTS FOR $100

ANSWER:
THE AGE A BABY GETS THEIR FIRST SHOT.

QUESTION:
WHAT IS TWO MONTHS?

CATEGORY: PEDIATRICIAN FOR $100

ANSWER:
A QUESTION TO ASK YOUR PEDIATRICIAN.

QUESTION:
WHAT IS FREQUENCY OF VISITS,
PROBABILITY OF ANOTHER PERSON
DELIVERING, ROLES OF ASSOCIATES,
PROCEDURE FOR TELEPHONED-IN
QUESTIONS, AVERAGE WAITING TIME FOR
AN APPOINTMENT?

CATEGORY: ARTS FOR $500

THIS CATEGORY INVOLVES THE PERFORMING ARTS! THE LUCKY PERSON GETS TO DRAW A PICTURE OF LIONS AND TIGERS AND BEARS USING CRAYONS ! OH MY! AND IT HAS TO BE FINISHED WITHIN 1 MINUTE!

CATEGORY: ?

PLACE A BET AND DOUBLE YOUR MONEY IF
YOUR TEAM WINS. COUNT OFF IN TWO
TEAMS AND TRY TO SOLVE THIS PUZZLE.
CHILDREN ARE _!

HOSTESS: GIVE EVERYONE PAPER AND
PENCIL AND LET THEM KNOW HOW MANY
LETTERS AND SPACES TO SOLVE THE
PUZZLE.

ANSWER :"THE REWARD OF LIFE!"

CATEGORY: STRESS FOR $300

STRESS IS WHEN YOU THOUGHT YOUR
BABY WAS EATING THE FOOD WHEN THEY
ARE ACTUALLY WEARING IT!
BLINDFOLD THE PERSON AND HAVE THEM
GUESS WHAT THEY ARE PUTTING THEIR
FINGER INTO!

HOSTESS: USE THREE CUPS AND FILL WITH
APPLESAUCE, FLOUR, AND OATMEAL.

CATEGORY: SLEEP FOR $200

QUESTION:
HOW MANY HOURS OF SLEEP DO NEW
PARENTS GET?

ANSWER:
IF YOU ANSWERED ANYTHING OTHER THAN
ZERO, THINK AGAIN!
TRY MINUTES AT A TIME!

CATEGORY: CULTURE FOR $500

QUESTION:
WHAT ARE SOME WAYS THAT A CHILD CAN
LEARN ABOUT THEIR CULTURE AND OTHER
CULTURES?

ANSWERS: GOING TO CULTURALLY
DIVERSE SCHOOLS, READING WITH
PARENTS, VISITING HISTORICAL MUSEUMS.
AND MUCH MORE!

CATEGORY: S

"SKIP" THE PERSON. GO TO THEIR RIGHT!

CATEGORY: P

THE LUCKY PERSON GETS TO PICK A GIFT!
(OR PICK A GIFT FOR THE MOTHER-TO-BE
TO OPEN!)

CATEGORY: FOOD FOR $100

QUESTION:
WHAT IS A SIMPLE WAY TO MAKE BATCHES OF BABY FOOD?

ANSWER:
MIX FRESH FRUITS AND VEGGIES IN THE BLENDER AND FREEZE THEM IN AN ICE CUBE TRAY. PUT THEM IN A DIVIDED COVERED BOWL IN THE DIAPER BAG. YOU HAVE A READY MADE MEAL FOR THE SITTER.

CATEGORY: TODDLER FOR $100

QUESTION:
AT WHAT AGE DOES CHILD DRINK WHOLE MILK?

ANSWER:
AT THE AGE OF 12 MONTHS.

CATEGORY: NAMES FOR $100

QUESTION:
STATE TWO NAMES THAT RHYME WITH
BOY!

ANSWER:
ROY, JOY

HEIGHT
&
WEIGHT

CATEGORY: HEIGHT & WEIGHT FOR $100

QUESTION:
HOW OFTEN SHOULD H&W BE RECORDED?

ANSWER:
EVERY MONTH.

CATEGORY: CAR SEATS FOR $100

QUESTION:
WHAT IS THE YOUNGEST AGE FOR A CAR
SEAT?

ANSWER :
FROM BIRTH.

CATEGORY: BABYSITTERS FOR $100

QUESTION:
WHAT IS AN IMPORTANT THING TO TELL
THE BABYSITTER?

ANSWER:
THE PHONE NUMBER TO REACH YOU,
EMERGENCY NUMBERS, BABY'S
SCHEDULE, SUPPLIES FOR CHANGING,
SPECIAL NEEDS FOR SLEEPING, AND
COMFORTING WHEN CRYING.

CATEGORY: DAYCARE FOR $100

ANSWER:
A QUESTION MOM SHOULD ASK OF A
DAYCARE CENTER?

QUESTION:
WHAT IS THE RATIO OF CAREGIVERS TO
INFANTS, CREDENTIALS, HOURS, IS
EQUIPMENT SAFE, FEEDING METHODS,
CLEANING METHODS, CAN YOU COME IN AT
ANY TIME, IS IT A NON SMOKING
ENVIRONMENT?

CATEGORY: WILD

PLACE A BET AND DOUBLE YOUR MONEY!
OR LOSE IT ALL IF YOU DON'T FIND THE
ITEMS WITHIN 2 MINUTES!
FIND THE TWO HIDDEN BABY ITEMS!

HOSTESS: LET THE PERSON KNOW IF THEY
ARE GETTING HOTTER OR COLDER WHEN
THEY ARE SEARCHING FOR THE HIDDEN
ITEMS!

CATEGORY: T FOR $200

TRY TO GET 13 COTTON BALLS INTO A
BOWL BY BLOWING THEM WITH A
BLINDFOLD OVER YOUR EYES. TIME LIMIT
OF 30 SECONDS.

NOTE: PLACE THE COTTON BALLS ON A
TABLE AND SIT THE PERSON AT THE TABLE
WITH THE BLINDFOLD ON. MOVE THE BOWL
TO CATCH ANY FALLING COTTON BALLS!

CATEGORY: DAD FOR $500

ANSWER:
THE MOST IMPORTANT THING FOR DAD TO
REMEMBER TO BUY BEFORE TAKING MOM
HOME FROM THE HOSPITAL.

QUESTION:
 WHAT ARE FLOWERS FOR MOM! ?

CATEGORY: SEX FOR $500

QUESTION:
WHAT DO YOU DO WHEN ROMANCE IS
MISSING AND THE BABY IS TAKING UP ALL
OF YOUR TIME?

ANSWER:
PLAN SOME TIME ALONE. DINNER, HOME
ALONE, A DATE, GET A SITTER!

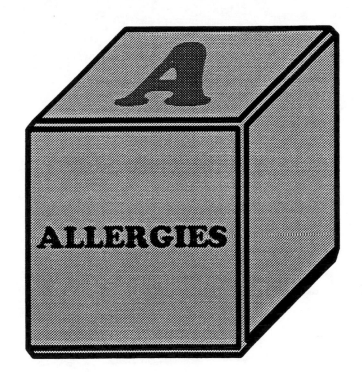

CATEGORY: ALLERGIES FOR $100

ANSWER:
TWO COMMON ALLERGIES CHILDREN
HAVE.

QUESTION:
WHAT ARE EGGS AND MILK?

CATEGORY: HELP! FOR $500

QUESTION:
NAME THE PERSON THAT DAD IS MOST
LIKELY TO CALL FOR "HELP" WHEN MOM
HAS THE DAY TO HERSELF AND HE HAS
THE BABY!

ANSWER:
HE WILL PROBABLY CALL HIS MOM!

CATEGORY: LOANS FOR $100

QUESTION:
IF YOU BORROW EQUIP WHAT SHOULD
YOU CHECK?

ANSWER:
DOES IT MEET CURRENT SAFETY
STANDARDS AND IS IT GENERALLY SAFE?

CATEGORY: DAYOUTING FOR $100

ANSWER:
AN ITEM TO INCLUDE WHEN GOING TO
DISNEYLAND.

QUESTION:
WHAT IS EXTRA DIAPERS, BOTTLES,
STROLLER, HAT, WIPES?

CATEGORY: STROLLERS FOR $100

ANSWER:
AN ACCESSORY ON A STROLLER.

QUESTION:
WHAT IS A BASKET, NET, CANOPY, OR SHIELD?

CATEGORY: GIRL FOR $200

QUESTION:
FINISH THIS SENTENCE: "GIRLS ARE MADE
OF ..."

ANSWER:
"SUGAR AND SPICE AND EVERYTHING
NICE!"

CATEGORY: OVERNIGHT FOR $100

ANSWER:
SOMETHING YOU TAKE OVERNIGHT FOR
THE BABY.

QUESTION:
WHAT IS CLOTHING, DIAPERS, BLANKET,
BOTTLES, WIPES, FOOD?

CATEGORY: EQUIPMENT FOR $100

QUESTION:
WHAT IS THE MOST IMPORTANT FACTOR
WHEN BUYING EQUIPMENT?

ANSWER:
THE SAFETY OF THE EQUIPMENT.

CATEGORY: BOY FOR $200

QUESTION:
LIST THREE BOY NAMES THAT RHYME
WITH SMILE!

ANSWER:
KYLE, LYLE, MILES.

CATEGORY: D FOR $500

ANSWER:
THE NUMBER OF "DAIRY" SERVINGS
RECOMMENDED DAILY DURING
PREGNANCY.

QUESTION:
WHAT IS 3-4 SERVINGS DAILY?

CATEGORY: BILLS FOR $300

QUESTION:
A GOOD WAY TO KEEP BILLS ORGANIZED
DURING THE ARRIVAL OF THE NEW BABY.
(BECAUSE YOU HAVE ENOUGH TO
REMEMBER!)

ANSWER:
BUY A BUDGET BOOK, USE A BOX OR
CONTAINER, USE YOUR COMPUTER, BUY
STAMPS AND ENVELOPES AHEAD OF TIME
AND FILE THEM BY DATE TO BE MAILED.

CATEGORY: CLOTHING FOR $200

QUESTION:
HOW DO YOU CHOOSE THE CLOTHING SIZE
FOR A CHILD?

ANSWER :
BY WEIGHT AND HEIGHT.

TOYS	LOVE	RELIGIOUS	NURSERY	CHILDREN'S BOOKS	TEENAGER
2	MEDITA-TION	L	FRIENDS	BOTTLES	LAYETTE
FORMULA	GRANDMA	HOSPITAL	WILD	SHOTS	PEDIA-TRICIAN
ARTS	?	STRESS	SLEEP	CULTURE	S
P	FOOD	TODDLER	NAMES	HEIGHT AND WEIGHT	CAR SEATS
BABY-SITTER	DAY CARE	WILD	T	DAD	SEX
ALLERGIES	HELP!	LOANS	DAY OUTING	STROLLER	GIRL
OVERNIGHT	EQUIP-MENT	BOY	D	BILLS	CLOTHING

BABY BLOCKS TALLY SHEET

GUEST NAME: _____

BABY DOLLARS $ _____
BABY DOLLARS $ _____
BABY DOLLARS $ _____
BABY DOLLARS $ _____
BABY DOLLARS $ _____
BABY DOLLARS $ _____
BABY DOLLARS $ _____
BABY DOLLARS $ _____
BABY DOLLARS $ _____
BABY DOLLARS $ _____
BABY DOLLARS $ _____
BABY DOLLARS $ _____

TOTAL $

TOYS	LOVE	RELIGIOUS	NURSERY	CHILDREN'S BOOKS	TEENAGER
2	MEDITA-TION	L	FRIENDS	BOTTLES	LAYETTE
FORMULA	GRANDMA	HOSPITAL	WILD	SHOTS	PEDIA-TRICIAN
ARTS	?	STRESS	SLEEP	CULTURE	S
P	FOOD	TODDLER	NAMES	HEIGHT AND WEIGHT	CAR SEATS
BABY-SITTER	DAY CARE	WILD	T	DAD	SEX
ALLERGIES	HELP!	LOANS	DAY OUTING	STROLLER	GIRL
OVERNIGHT	EQUIP-MENT	BOY	D	BILLS	CLOTHING

BABY BLOCKS TALLY SHEET

GUEST NAME: _____

BABY DOLLARS $ _____
BABY DOLLARS $ _____
BABY DOLLARS $ _____
BABY DOLLARS $ _____
BABY DOLLARS $ _____
BABY DOLLARS $ _____
BABY DOLLARS $ _____
BABY DOLLARS $ _____
BABY DOLLARS $ _____
BABY DOLLARS $ _____
BABY DOLLARS $ _____
BABY DOLLARS $ _____

TOTAL $

TOYS	LOVE	RELIGIOUS	NURSERY	CHILDREN'S BOOKS	TEENAGER
2	MEDITA-TION	L	FRIENDS	BOTTLES	LAYETTE
FORMULA	GRANDMA	HOSPITAL	WILD	SHOTS	PEDIA-TRICIAN
ARTS	?	STRESS	SLEEP	CULTURE	S
P	FOOD	TODDLER	NAMES	HEIGHT AND WEIGHT	CAR SEATS
BABY-SITTER	DAY CARE	WILD	T	DAD	SEX
ALLERGIES	HELP!	LOANS	DAY OUTING	STROLLER	GIRL
OVERNIGHT	EQUIP-MENT	BOY	D	BILLS	CLOTHING

BABY BLOCKS TALLY SHEET

GUEST NAME: _____

BABY DOLLARS $ _____
BABY DOLLARS $ _____
BABY DOLLARS $ _____
BABY DOLLARS $ _____
BABY DOLLARS $ _____
BABY DOLLARS $ _____
BABY DOLLARS $ _____
BABY DOLLARS $ _____
BABY DOLLARS $ _____
BABY DOLLARS $ _____
BABY DOLLARS $ _____
BABY DOLLARS $ _____

TOTAL $

TOYS	LOVE	RELIGIOUS	NURSERY	CHILDREN'S BOOKS	TEENAGER
2	MEDITA-TION	L	FRIENDS	BOTTLES	LAYETTE
FORMULA	GRANDMA	HOSPITAL	WILD	SHOTS	PEDIA-TRICIAN
ARTS	?	STRESS	SLEEP	CULTURE	S
P	FOOD	TODDLER	NAMES	HEIGHT AND WEIGHT	CAR SEATS
BABY-SITTER	DAY CARE	WILD	T	DAD	SEX
ALLERGIES	HELP!	LOANS	DAY OUTING	STROLLER	GIRL
OVERNIGHT	EQUIP-MENT	BOY	D	BILLS	CLOTHING

BABY BLOCKS TALLY SHEET

GUEST NAME: _____

BABY DOLLARS $ _____
BABY DOLLARS $ _____
BABY DOLLARS $ _____
BABY DOLLARS $ _____
BABY DOLLARS $ _____
BABY DOLLARS $ _____
BABY DOLLARS $ _____
BABY DOLLARS $ _____
BABY DOLLARS $ _____
BABY DOLLARS $ _____
BABY DOLLARS $ _____
BABY DOLLARS $ _____

TOTAL $

TOYS	LOVE	RELIGIOUS	NURSERY	CHILDREN'S BOOKS	TEENAGER
2	MEDITA-TION	L	FRIENDS	BOTTLES	LAYETTE
FORMULA	GRANDMA	HOSPITAL	WILD	SHOTS	PEDIA-TRICIAN
ARTS	?	STRESS	SLEEP	CULTURE	S
P	FOOD	TODDLER	NAMES	HEIGHT AND WEIGHT	CAR SEATS
BABY-SITTER	DAY CARE	WILD	T	DAD	SEX
ALLERGIES	HELP!	LOANS	DAY OUTING	STROLLER	GIRL
OVERNIGHT	EQUIP-MENT	BOY	D	BILLS	CLOTHING

BABY BLOCKS TALLY SHEET

GUEST NAME: _____

BABY DOLLARS $ _____
BABY DOLLARS $ _____
BABY DOLLARS $ _____
BABY DOLLARS $ _____
BABY DOLLARS $ _____
BABY DOLLARS $ _____
BABY DOLLARS $ _____
BABY DOLLARS $ _____
BABY DOLLARS $ _____
BABY DOLLARS $ _____
BABY DOLLARS $ _____
BABY DOLLARS $ _____

TOTAL $

TOYS	LOVE	RELIGIOUS	NURSERY	CHILDREN'S BOOKS	TEENAGER
2	MEDITA-TION	L	FRIENDS	BOTTLES	LAYETTE
FORMULA	GRANDMA	HOSPITAL	WILD	SHOTS	PEDIA-TRICIAN
ARTS	?	STRESS	SLEEP	CULTURE	S
P	FOOD	TODDLER	NAMES	HEIGHT AND WEIGHT	CAR SEATS
BABY-SITTER	DAY CARE	WILD	T	DAD	SEX
ALLERGIES	HELP!	LOANS	DAY OUTING	STROLLER	GIRL
OVERNIGHT	EQUIP-MENT	BOY	D	BILLS	CLOTHING

BABY BLOCKS TALLY SHEET

GUEST NAME: _____

BABY DOLLARS $ _____
BABY DOLLARS $ _____
BABY DOLLARS $ _____
BABY DOLLARS $ _____
BABY DOLLARS $ _____
BABY DOLLARS $ _____
BABY DOLLARS $ _____
BABY DOLLARS $ _____
BABY DOLLARS $ _____
BABY DOLLARS $ _____
BABY DOLLARS $ _____
BABY DOLLARS $ _____

TOTAL $

TOYS	LOVE	RELIGIOUS	NURSERY	CHILDREN'S BOOKS	TEENAGER
2	MEDITA-TION	L	FRIENDS	BOTTLES	LAYETTE
FORMULA	GRANDMA	HOSPITAL	WILD	SHOTS	PEDIA-TRICIAN
ARTS	?	STRESS	SLEEP	CULTURE	S
P	FOOD	TODDLER	NAMES	HEIGHT AND WEIGHT	CAR SEATS
BABY-SITTER	DAY CARE	WILD	T	DAD	SEX
ALLERGIES	HELP!	LOANS	DAY OUTING	STROLLER	GIRL
OVERNIGHT	EQUIP-MENT	BOY	D	BILLS	CLOTHING

BABY BLOCKS TALLY SHEET

GUEST NAME: _____

BABY DOLLARS $ _____
BABY DOLLARS $ _____
BABY DOLLARS $ _____
BABY DOLLARS $ _____
BABY DOLLARS $ _____
BABY DOLLARS $ _____
BABY DOLLARS $ _____
BABY DOLLARS $ _____
BABY DOLLARS $ _____
BABY DOLLARS $ _____
BABY DOLLARS $ _____
BABY DOLLARS $ _____

TOTAL $

TOYS	LOVE	RELIGIOUS	NURSERY	CHILDREN'S BOOKS	TEENAGER
2	MEDITA-TION	L	FRIENDS	BOTTLES	LAYETTE
FORMULA	GRANDMA	HOSPITAL	WILD	SHOTS	PEDIA-TRICIAN
ARTS	?	STRESS	SLEEP	CULTURE	S
P	FOOD	TODDLER	NAMES	HEIGHT AND WEIGHT	CAR SEATS
BABY-SITTER	DAY CARE	WILD	T	DAD	SEX
ALLERGIES	HELP!	LOANS	DAY OUTING	STROLLER	GIRL
OVERNIGHT	EQUIP-MENT	BOY	D	BILLS	CLOTHING

BABY BLOCKS TALLY SHEET

GUEST NAME: _____

BABY DOLLARS $ _____
BABY DOLLARS $ _____
BABY DOLLARS $ _____
BABY DOLLARS $ _____
BABY DOLLARS $ _____
BABY DOLLARS $ _____
BABY DOLLARS $ _____
BABY DOLLARS $ _____
BABY DOLLARS $ _____
BABY DOLLARS $ _____
BABY DOLLARS $ _____
BABY DOLLARS $ _____

TOTAL $

TOYS	LOVE	RELIGIOUS	NURSERY	CHILDREN'S BOOKS	TEENAGER
2	MEDITA-TION	L	FRIENDS	BOTTLES	LAYETTE
FORMULA	GRANDMA	HOSPITAL	WILD	SHOTS	PEDIA-TRICIAN
ARTS	?	STRESS	SLEEP	CULTURE	S
P	FOOD	TODDLER	NAMES	HEIGHT AND WEIGHT	CAR SEATS
BABY-SITTER	DAY CARE	WILD	T	DAD	SEX
ALLERGIES	HELP!	LOANS	DAY OUTING	STROLLER	GIRL
OVERNIGHT	EQUIP-MENT	BOY	D	BILLS	CLOTHING

BABY BLOCKS TALLY SHEET

GUEST NAME: _____

BABY DOLLARS $ _____
BABY DOLLARS $ _____
BABY DOLLARS $ _____
BABY DOLLARS $ _____
BABY DOLLARS $ _____
BABY DOLLARS $ _____
BABY DOLLARS $ _____
BABY DOLLARS $ _____
BABY DOLLARS $ _____
BABY DOLLARS $ _____
BABY DOLLARS $ _____
BABY DOLLARS $ _____

TOTAL $

TOYS	LOVE	RELIGIOUS	NURSERY	CHILDREN'S BOOKS	TEENAGER
2	MEDITA-TION	L	FRIENDS	BOTTLES	LAYETTE
FORMULA	GRANDMA	HOSPITAL	WILD	SHOTS	PEDIA-TRICIAN
ARTS	?	STRESS	SLEEP	CULTURE	S
P	FOOD	TODDLER	NAMES	HEIGHT AND WEIGHT	CAR SEATS
BABY-SITTER	DAY CARE	WILD	T	DAD	SEX
ALLERGIES	HELP!	LOANS	DAY OUTING	STROLLER	GIRL
OVERNIGHT	EQUIP-MENT	BOY	D	BILLS	CLOTHING

BABY BLOCKS TALLY SHEET

GUEST NAME: _____

BABY DOLLARS $ _____
BABY DOLLARS $ _____
BABY DOLLARS $ _____
BABY DOLLARS $ _____
BABY DOLLARS $ _____
BABY DOLLARS $ _____
BABY DOLLARS $ _____
BABY DOLLARS $ _____
BABY DOLLARS $ _____
BABY DOLLARS $ _____
BABY DOLLARS $ _____
BABY DOLLARS $ _____

TOTAL $

TOYS	LOVE	RELIGIOUS	NURSERY	CHILDREN'S BOOKS	TEENAGER
2	MEDITA-TION	L	FRIENDS	BOTTLES	LAYETTE
FORMULA	GRANDMA	HOSPITAL	WILD	SHOTS	PEDIA-TRICIAN
ARTS	?	STRESS	SLEEP	CULTURE	S
P	FOOD	TODDLER	NAMES	HEIGHT AND WEIGHT	CAR SEATS
BABY-SITTER	DAY CARE	WILD	T	DAD	SEX
ALLERGIES	HELP!	LOANS	DAY OUTING	STROLLER	GIRL
OVERNIGHT	EQUIP-MENT	BOY	D	BILLS	CLOTHING

BABY BLOCKS TALLY SHEET

GUEST NAME: _____

BABY DOLLARS $ _____
BABY DOLLARS $ _____
BABY DOLLARS $ _____
BABY DOLLARS $ _____
BABY DOLLARS $ _____
BABY DOLLARS $ _____
BABY DOLLARS $ _____
BABY DOLLARS $ _____
BABY DOLLARS $ _____
BABY DOLLARS $ _____
BABY DOLLARS $ _____
BABY DOLLARS $ _____

TOTAL $

TOYS	LOVE	RELIGIOUS	NURSERY	CHILDREN'S BOOKS	TEENAGER
2	MEDITA-TION	L	FRIENDS	BOTTLES	LAYETTE
FORMULA	GRANDMA	HOSPITAL	WILD	SHOTS	PEDIA-TRICIAN
ARTS	?	STRESS	SLEEP	CULTURE	S
P	FOOD	TODDLER	NAMES	HEIGHT AND WEIGHT	CAR SEATS
BABY-SITTER	DAY CARE	WILD	T	DAD	SEX
ALLERGIES	HELP!	LOANS	DAY OUTING	STROLLER	GIRL
OVERNIGHT	EQUIP-MENT	BOY	D	BILLS	CLOTHING

BABY BLOCKS TALLY SHEET

GUEST NAME: _____

BABY DOLLARS $ _____
BABY DOLLARS $ _____
BABY DOLLARS $ _____
BABY DOLLARS $ _____
BABY DOLLARS $ _____
BABY DOLLARS $ _____
BABY DOLLARS $ _____
BABY DOLLARS $ _____
BABY DOLLARS $ _____
BABY DOLLARS $ _____
BABY DOLLARS $ _____
BABY DOLLARS $ _____

TOTAL $

TOYS	LOVE	RELIGIOUS	NURSERY	CHILDREN'S BOOKS	TEENAGER
2	MEDITA-TION	L	FRIENDS	BOTTLES	LAYETTE
FORMULA	GRANDMA	HOSPITAL	WILD	SHOTS	PEDIA-TRICIAN
ARTS	?	STRESS	SLEEP	CULTURE	S
P	FOOD	TODDLER	NAMES	HEIGHT AND WEIGHT	CAR SEATS
BABY-SITTER	DAY CARE	WILD	T	DAD	SEX
ALLERGIES	HELP!	LOANS	DAY OUTING	STROLLER	GIRL
OVERNIGHT	EQUIP-MENT	BOY	D	BILLS	CLOTHING

BABY BLOCKS TALLY SHEET

GUEST NAME: _____

BABY DOLLARS $ _____
BABY DOLLARS $ _____
BABY DOLLARS $ _____
BABY DOLLARS $ _____
BABY DOLLARS $ _____
BABY DOLLARS $ _____
BABY DOLLARS $ _____
BABY DOLLARS $ _____
BABY DOLLARS $ _____
BABY DOLLARS $ _____
BABY DOLLARS $ _____
BABY DOLLARS $ _____

TOTAL $

TOYS	LOVE	RELIGIOUS	NURSERY	CHILDREN'S BOOKS	TEENAGER
2	MEDITA-TION	L	FRIENDS	BOTTLES	LAYETTE
FORMULA	GRANDMA	HOSPITAL	WILD	SHOTS	PEDIA-TRICIAN
ARTS	?	STRESS	SLEEP	CULTURE	S
P	FOOD	TODDLER	NAMES	HEIGHT AND WEIGHT	CAR SEATS
BABY-SITTER	DAY CARE	WILD	T	DAD	SEX
ALLERGIES	HELP!	LOANS	DAY OUTING	STROLLER	GIRL
OVERNIGHT	EQUIP-MENT	BOY	D	BILLS	CLOTHING

BABY BLOCKS TALLY SHEET

GUEST NAME: _____

BABY DOLLARS $ _____
BABY DOLLARS $ _____
BABY DOLLARS $ _____
BABY DOLLARS $ _____
BABY DOLLARS $ _____
BABY DOLLARS $ _____
BABY DOLLARS $ _____
BABY DOLLARS $ _____
BABY DOLLARS $ _____
BABY DOLLARS $ _____
BABY DOLLARS $ _____
BABY DOLLARS $ _____

TOTAL $

TOYS	LOVE	RELIGIOUS	NURSERY	CHILDREN'S BOOKS	TEENAGER
2	MEDITA-TION	L	FRIENDS	BOTTLES	LAYETTE
FORMULA	GRANDMA	HOSPITAL	WILD	SHOTS	PEDIA-TRICIAN
ARTS	?	STRESS	SLEEP	CULTURE	S
P	FOOD	TODDLER	NAMES	HEIGHT AND WEIGHT	CAR SEATS
BABY-SITTER	DAY CARE	WILD	T	DAD	SEX
ALLERGIES	HELP!	LOANS	DAY OUTING	STROLLER	GIRL
OVERNIGHT	EQUIP-MENT	BOY	D	BILLS	CLOTHING

BABY BLOCKS TALLY SHEET

GUEST NAME: _____

BABY DOLLARS $ _____
BABY DOLLARS $ _____
BABY DOLLARS $ _____
BABY DOLLARS $ _____
BABY DOLLARS $ _____
BABY DOLLARS $ _____
BABY DOLLARS $ _____
BABY DOLLARS $ _____
BABY DOLLARS $ _____
BABY DOLLARS $ _____
BABY DOLLARS $ _____
BABY DOLLARS $ _____

TOTAL $

TOYS	LOVE	RELIGIOUS	NURSERY	CHILDREN'S BOOKS	TEENAGER
2	MEDITA-TION	L	FRIENDS	BOTTLES	LAYETTE
FORMULA	GRANDMA	HOSPITAL	WILD	SHOTS	PEDIA-TRICIAN
ARTS	?	STRESS	SLEEP	CULTURE	S
P	FOOD	TODDLER	NAMES	HEIGHT AND WEIGHT	CAR SEATS
BABY-SITTER	DAY CARE	WILD	T	DAD	SEX
ALLERGIES	HELP!	LOANS	DAY OUTING	STROLLER	GIRL
OVERNIGHT	EQUIP-MENT	BOY	D	BILLS	CLOTHING

BABY BLOCKS TALLY SHEET

GUEST NAME: _____

BABY DOLLARS $ _____
BABY DOLLARS $ _____
BABY DOLLARS $ _____
BABY DOLLARS $ _____
BABY DOLLARS $ _____
BABY DOLLARS $ _____
BABY DOLLARS $ _____
BABY DOLLARS $ _____
BABY DOLLARS $ _____
BABY DOLLARS $ _____
BABY DOLLARS $ _____
BABY DOLLARS $ _____

TOTAL $

TOYS	LOVE	RELIGIOUS	NURSERY	CHILDREN'S BOOKS	TEENAGER
2	MEDITA-TION	L	FRIENDS	BOTTLES	LAYETTE
FORMULA	GRANDMA	HOSPITAL	WILD	SHOTS	PEDIA-TRICIAN
ARTS	?	STRESS	SLEEP	CULTURE	S
P	FOOD	TODDLER	NAMES	HEIGHT AND WEIGHT	CAR SEATS
BABY-SITTER	DAY CARE	WILD	T	DAD	SEX
ALLERGIES	HELP!	LOANS	DAY OUTING	STROLLER	GIRL
OVERNIGHT	EQUIP-MENT	BOY	D	BILLS	CLOTHING

BABY BLOCKS TALLY SHEET

GUEST NAME: _____

BABY DOLLARS $ _____
BABY DOLLARS $ _____
BABY DOLLARS $ _____
BABY DOLLARS $ _____
BABY DOLLARS $ _____
BABY DOLLARS $ _____
BABY DOLLARS $ _____
BABY DOLLARS $ _____
BABY DOLLARS $ _____
BABY DOLLARS $ _____
BABY DOLLARS $ _____
BABY DOLLARS $ _____

TOTAL $

TOYS	LOVE	RELIGIOUS	NURSERY	CHILDREN'S BOOKS	TEENAGER
2	MEDITA-TION	L	FRIENDS	BOTTLES	LAYETTE
FORMULA	GRANDMA	HOSPITAL	WILD	SHOTS	PEDIA-TRICIAN
ARTS	?	STRESS	SLEEP	CULTURE	S
P	FOOD	TODDLER	NAMES	HEIGHT AND WEIGHT	CAR SEATS
BABY-SITTER	DAY CARE	WILD	T	DAD	SEX
ALLERGIES	HELP!	LOANS	DAY OUTING	STROLLER	GIRL
OVERNIGHT	EQUIP-MENT	BOY	D	BILLS	CLOTHING

BABY BLOCKS TALLY SHEET

GUEST NAME: _____

BABY DOLLARS $ _____
BABY DOLLARS $ _____
BABY DOLLARS $ _____
BABY DOLLARS $ _____
BABY DOLLARS $ _____
BABY DOLLARS $ _____
BABY DOLLARS $ _____
BABY DOLLARS $ _____
BABY DOLLARS $ _____
BABY DOLLARS $ _____
BABY DOLLARS $ _____
BABY DOLLARS $ _____

TOTAL $

TOYS	LOVE	RELIGIOUS	NURSERY	CHILDREN'S BOOKS	TEENAGER
2	MEDITA-TION	L	FRIENDS	BOTTLES	LAYETTE
FORMULA	GRANDMA	HOSPITAL	WILD	SHOTS	PEDIA-TRICIAN
ARTS	?	STRESS	SLEEP	CULTURE	S
P	FOOD	TODDLER	NAMES	HEIGHT AND WEIGHT	CAR SEATS
BABY-SITTER	DAY CARE	WILD	T	DAD	SEX
ALLERGIES	HELP!	LOANS	DAY OUTING	STROLLER	GIRL
OVERNIGHT	EQUIP-MENT	BOY	D	BILLS	CLOTHING

BABY BLOCKS TALLY SHEET

GUEST NAME: _____

BABY DOLLARS $ _____
BABY DOLLARS $ _____
BABY DOLLARS $ _____
BABY DOLLARS $ _____
BABY DOLLARS $ _____
BABY DOLLARS $ _____
BABY DOLLARS $ _____
BABY DOLLARS $ _____
BABY DOLLARS $ _____
BABY DOLLARS $ _____
BABY DOLLARS $ _____
BABY DOLLARS $ _____

TOTAL $

TOYS	LOVE	RELIGIOUS	NURSERY	CHILDREN'S BOOKS	TEENAGER
2	MEDITA-TION	L	FRIENDS	BOTTLES	LAYETTE
FORMULA	GRANDMA	HOSPITAL	WILD	SHOTS	PEDIA-TRICIAN
ARTS	?	STRESS	SLEEP	CULTURE	S
P	FOOD	TODDLER	NAMES	HEIGHT AND WEIGHT	CAR SEATS
BABY-SITTER	DAY CARE	WILD	T	DAD	SEX
ALLERGIES	HELP!	LOANS	DAY OUTING	STROLLER	GIRL
OVERNIGHT	EQUIP-MENT	BOY	D	BILLS	CLOTHING

BABY BLOCKS TALLY SHEET

GUEST NAME: _____

BABY DOLLARS $ _____
BABY DOLLARS $ _____
BABY DOLLARS $ _____
BABY DOLLARS $ _____
BABY DOLLARS $ _____
BABY DOLLARS $ _____
BABY DOLLARS $ _____
BABY DOLLARS $ _____
BABY DOLLARS $ _____
BABY DOLLARS $ _____
BABY DOLLARS $ _____
BABY DOLLARS $ _____

TOTAL $